I dedicate these works to my beautiful wife.

I love you Kylie.

Hunger

I draw to her fair skinned succulous neck
Vampiric urges to put my lips upon thee
Not to bite but a kiss, moist and gentle as dew
Petrified by her eyes as they survey the surroundings
Invisible as if I stand in the corner by shadows
Clocks lack their tick, flowers grow in her presence
While their scents follow her breeze upon exit
If I could grasp words to express her pure beauty
She would collapse in my arms and love so exquisite
I will always remember the first time she left me
Striving for the day when silence may be broken
Alone I shall wait, ponder and daze.

Join

I lay and cover her body with mine
My knees rest neatly below her thighs
Clutched with one arm from waist to neck
Content as we share a fresh cigarette
I nestle closer, an inch at a time
She does the same, her body with mine

As She Dances

The effervescent actions of that luscious colleen
Spry and nimble I observed as a glutton
The envy of her peers and all vigilant eyes
Effortlessly adroit as if born from grandeur
Her svelte silhouette is imprinted in my eyes
Like flashing dots after an extended glare at the sun
I squint and blink to regain my equilibrium
Swilling Scotch neat from a short glass, my vigil

Careless Avowal

Unvalued she works
Striving for intangible perfection
Blood sweat and tears saturate her drive
Motivation never wanes or looses intensity
Forgiving but stern with command
Mental celebrations are the jubilee
Thanks are not given to the women
Though assumptions are a plenty
Lost labors surely shift the axis
Perception would be quickly found
I beg forgiveness my love
Beholden to you we orbit

Bear no Malice

Sun missed roseate lips, thin and taut as if to kiss.
Hair that flows despair to those encouraged will remiss.
Though ones who only know will go and struggle with a fist.
Love overflows to not oppose foes keeping a long list.
Those with woes will go to show their friend the cuttlefish.
Bestow grace and glory as a gift, leave others left to wish.

Awake I will Stay

I wake and behold yonder to beside beauty.
Not knowing of my groggy eyes upon thee.
Fresh from slumber but radiant as the night.
Her milky skin shines in the rays of morning.
If it was realized the bounty before me,
She might flee as from a ravenous beast.
In the interim she is motionless, still unaware of my gaze.
My own secret Venus de Milo, a masterwork of the heavens.
I give thanks, glory and praise for felicity.
Overwhelmed, a slight pinch to test my inquisition.
As if listening to my inner dialog she twists in my direction,
with her eyes over shoulder.
Three soft, sweet words roll from her lips.
My dear, blessed in her grace, awake I will stay.

As She Smirks

I fumble for my drink and graze her knee.
An intentional accident it seems.
Daydreaming of the denouement.
Her stare questions my motivation.
My actions are my worst enemy.
I'm transparent, awkward and obvious.
She seems amused and comfortable.
The turned corners of her mouth form a smirk.
At that very moment I understand story's told.
I've lost the sweat from my palms.
They're warm and no longer clammy.
Her eyes sparkle reflecting the sun.
It can almost feel the heat.
The first impressions of my heart.

I Long for the Ocean

I long for the ocean
The orchestral sounds of nature
To hear the waves crashing like cymbals
Wake to the song of indigenous friends
I grow envious of the Pied Kingfisher as I sit empty hooked
He glances over, almost to mock me
Then dives once more and then quickly to surface
Straight into the clouds and off with his spoils
Sand conforms around my legs as I loosen
Fresh breeze from the gulf, I cannot move a muscle
I watch the sun melt into water at dusk
I will sleep well this eve and have dreams of the morrow

Technologically Savvy

Equipped for the future, transistorized with lies
You travel with sutures; they just curtain your eyes
From student to tutor, mime seismic failed tries
Look ahead young computer, with drives open, wise
Thoughts preserved in pewter, programmed metallic cries
Reality in a stupor while our history slowly dies

Serene Queen

Candy kisses, sweet delicious, closed eye for grand seen wishes Randi Mrs., dancing listless, experiment like Petri dishes. Commence lightly, soft politely, anticipate almost nightly. Intense and mighty, lustful feisty, incarnate of Aphrodite. A porous dream, intriguing screams, back and forth to in between. Torus rings, and shiny things, until death my serene queen.

The Beach

Fingers yellow gold from mellow smoke rolled. Incinerate from tips of ruby embers to my lips. Relax and gaze away with moonlit breeze and waves of grey. Old liquids pour, swish, smell, kiss. Cool sensation well accompanied by adoration. Hypnotized by visions of the sea, calmness right before I sleep.

Strife

Whispering tragedy and sporadic equality.
False pretenses to make them fond of me.
Darkness envelops and eludes mortality.
Ulterior motives that can defy gravity.
Reasons for shame, they're all the same.
Prescriptions for pain or to keep you insane.
Anger exudes fixations amuse.
Strife but aloof with quarrelling fools.

Overzealous

Overzealous in my stare
Though impossible to advert
This could remain my eternity
Complacent while visions don't fade
Other senses seem exaggerated
Your touch could shift my axis
Philosophies reform as opinions melt
Catawampus by cerebral gambits once again

Sweet Dreams

We share dreams of purity, everlasting and true.
Ideas of serenity fill my thoughts. Give and receive.
Calmness of post showers sweet nectar rain. Flowers and
spring. Our hearts are eternities that slumber with me.

Passion

Stars start to twinkle as blue skies float by.
Bodies entangled, caress hips and thighs.
Lips pressed against neck, mouth wide with surprise.
Her back gently expands to ease him inside.
Shrieks of passion, souls connect through two eyes.
Time tends to stop while all sounds mesmerize.
Affection is mighty and futile to fight.
Those in true love can indeed sympathize.
Unions are sacred as babes cry in the night.
Two become one and are full of delight.

Roll Over

Love nostalgia she shares my bed and heart
I awake pillow taken with a groggy smirk
Nudged into the small of my back I avoid knees
It's impossible as she squirms even closer than before
Though hot, uncomfortable and without room
I could never slumber in her absence

Poor Birthday

Festivities in the morrow quickly approach
Distraught as I broach my financial reproach
Shall I steal and sin to bring joy to another
My cheerful lover and children's mother
I could try and create the works of a master
With time against me, the outcome disaster
I pine to provide all the dreams of her mind
Though all she wants is the love by her side
I create ashes from art to smear on a canvas

<u>My darling</u>

I keep her sequestered from astringent actuality.
Her enormous heart is too delicate for reality.
She bleeds with love for the feelings of others.
The overwhelming compassion only felt by mothers.
Thoughts could change worlds and all children fed.
I will dream of the future with a kiss on my head.

<u>She</u>

She's my sun, my air and the beats of my heart.
She's my spring, my drive, my art.
She's my touch, my lust supplying me with power.
She's my love, my rock, my ivory tower.
For all of these things that she is to me
I only pray that she can see one of these things in me.

Sanguine

Encompassed souls, thoughts, feelings and dreams.
Process ever present but it is seldom seen.
Resolution is objective, memories affected.
Peering through experience from another time collected.
I'm sanguine, hoping for the same friend.
Alas, I just woke up from dreams at times that seem so ancient. Present is never stagnant, it's alive without compassion. With oar to water, row your boat to goals you cannot ration. Persistence is a fickle gift that's full of fear and fraction. When she believes and holds you close, you're washed in calmly fashion.

Matrimony

My nectar, and serendipitous comfort,
she rests in my arms as I thirst no longer.
Astonished smirk, face ruby with fluster,
awake but full of reverie I resolve my tomorrow.
Godly alliance, hands join in unison,
prose spoken from hearts now bound forever.
Glowing smile, Songbirds sing as in choir,
nuptials complete as we bask in the splendor.

Seasons

Whimsical winter winds whistle away to songbirds of spring, sweet serenade.
The Hot humid summer to waters we plunder till acorns of trees beat down like a drummer.
All year around the beauty and sounds.
They go by as fast as we spin round and round.
Spend with your love or spend with your friend.
Never melancholy because we will see you again.

Surreal Anguish

Light snow covers the ground like ash from ignited memories past. Last I might, or must to overthrow merciless dictators imagined. Flattened by the bone chilling cold, I'll curl up and die with my heat. Drumbeat hearts echo through canals of decomposed dreams. Themes of the malcontent youth flourish through alleyways often. Coffin filled courtyards towns surround, friends of whistled wind. Rescind from melancholy demeanor if able though despoiled. Oiled tungsten lanterns line parapets illuminating a blank canvas. Janus, lead me. Open stones for my escape to evaporate in the night. Light snow covers the ground like ash from ignited memories past.

Purpose

Purpose is given like untying a ribbon.
Neat and ornate as the lives we are living.
Meat from a hunt or grain from a harvest.
The fruits of our labor and dearly departed.
Astute in the mind but weak in the heart.
I seem to finish before I can start.

Jubilation

You encapsulate me like a grounded force.
Though ridiculous I retort.
Treating love like game or sport.
But everyone wins when holding soul bound friends.
In your grasp I breathe,
unknowing to the sea's that soon we will be part of them
feeling the breeze.
While the waves crash and my heart goes pitter pat
I'll always long for the day that I can have you back.
Without you I'm hollow and on the brink of insane.
As rain falls from my eyes in thunder storms of pain.
I miss the beach, when happiness was in reach.
Actions could be different with jubilation for each.

Vacant Magnificence

Her deliquescing dreams form salty streaks upon a cheek.
Once obsessed with eminence, to brave summits, any peak.
A sobbing somber serenade sings dreams alas you sleep.
The true nightmare lays awake, a calamity as you weep.
Futures change while past deranged as quickly as you blink.
Clouded mind, transparent eyes, stolen thoughts you think.

Our Life Together

She was nimble to conquer my thought
Complacent, pondering future memories
I reminiscence of tomorrow in lucidity
Such works tend to provoke my demeanor
Past and present tend to boggle the layman
Her allegiance drives a courageous shift
More is visible with the lack of mirrors
For what's abaft is irrelevant to your aim

Holy

Fountains of memories purge my subconscious.
Undisclosed locations and secret monuments.
I can only recall the horrific thoughts,
No laughter or happiness, equilibriums taught.
Can my smiles be resurrected?
Is reminiscing segregated?
Help me overcome this insanity.
Lord I know he's mad at me.
I follow the path naturally without blasphemy.
But he still boasts.
Turn water to wine and let's toast to our oaths.

Have Some

O young offender, dumb and ginger, again you go out on a bender. Thoughts you hinder while poisons render, in a gutter beneath a fender. Once from wealth and full of splendor, empty pockets, wallet slender. From the first time that you kissed her, to your lips a sweet elixir. One true love, you'll always miss her, grab a bottle and a mixer.

Slainte!

Logic

Futuristic fantasy's with out of body odysseys.
Obscure oddities boggle monosyllabically.
Bottled up wishes with dreams of winning lotteries.
Unreal investments, returns are more like robberies.
Don't liquidate lucidity to be paralyzed by property.
Explanation is futile; your logic doesn't bother me.

Little Old Man

Sweet little old man wrinkled from toe to hand.
The things that you've seen and places you can.
O stories you tell and wishes of well.
Beautiful things to violence like hell.
Will it be lost when you pay the cost?
Or fables to speak while kids lick the frost.

Growing

Eyes sparkle like gems of rare descent.
Exuberant eruptions of passion to present.
Like a present, gifts of joy, trust and consent.
Ever pleasant, lifts a boy to levels of no descent.
The child has grown, now it's time, innocent must repent.
From raucous rascals transformation to an intellectual gent.
Like wines that age and levels that raise, smell the grapes ferment. With cash and coin your time is lost not knowing what was spent. But if you spend it holding love your loss will be torment.

Sensation

Sensations deluge with your ubiquitous adoration.
Lackadaisical infatuation heartfelt and complacent.
Racing for evolution destinations adjacent.
Attainment is imminent with sacchariferous patience.

Her Embrace

Your embrace heats my soul like the sunrise on a Mediterranean mezzanine.
In your absence I speak an adoring soliloquy of longing to hold you so close to me.
Hands in hair, breast pressed neatly to chest, your breath in my ear in a song none the less.
Lips on your cheek gently kiss and caress while my knees enervated as I move to your neck.
My sweet seraph untamed and not embarrassed.
Encompassed by love and thoughts to never disparage.

To Haunt my Love

Daylight disappears before content.
No longer to behold your lineaments.
The return of my dim retribution.
I stir, only to wake in luster…confusion.
Rejoice, my sculpture of perfection.
I observe through empty eyes of deception.
My rest is hampered by her allegory.
Free me from this purgatory.
I saudade for her caress and kiss.
Let me be forgotten…unmissed.

Delicious

She is a wonderful listener
My lips tend to move faster than my breath
I'm left flustered and embarrassed
A kiss on the forehead calms me
All the while brushing the hair out of my eyes
She wants a clear look into my soul
To grasp what I really am
She already knows more than I intended
In her arms I have no control
Cradled like a babe, breasts in my face
I nestle closer as if to shield from the sunlight
She smells of Jasmine and Vanilla
Take a bite I ponder…I could
The effect wouldn't be worth the cause
Though I wonder

One

Entangled emotion with overflowing devotion.
One life, one chance, one love.
Restraint unforeseen in the eyes of a queen.
One wife, one glance, one hug.
Euphoric recollection with bursts of affection.
One night, one romance, one drug.

Comfort

O glorious, one of plentiful softness,
expand as I kiss and utter intangible passions.
My warmth, it's yours for the taking;
immersed in your existence I will never be naked.
Grips of flesh, nimble but vigorous hustle,
peerless delight as we meld in one another's confidence.
Nestled strong, having irrevocable practice,
I slumber pining for your art and with embrace I awaken.

Writers Block

Lacking inspiration
In need of a gala to crush me
Bring me back to the levels that I once was accustom
Infused with boredom
While I sleep I grow tired
As the wild one screams, pitter pat with the moon
A contentious daze
Dare they disturb my boggle
I am far too subdued with retort for insanity
White knuckled
An ignorant inventor

Empathy

Optimistic sentiments, irrelevant but negligent
Observers sit like sediment. Snakes, they lurk intelligent
Looks through slits of eyes, incapable surprise
You idolize and socialize, They smack flies, families die
Empathy is vaporized. I will startle and shake foundations
Uproot imaginations as we all scream salvation
Hands moist, forehead a glaze. I long for fires lit ablaze
Burn these things that are all the craze
Your lazy days can drift away
Technology speaks to those of prey.

Indefinable Felicity

A glorious spirit, angelic, utopian
Surpassed only by souls metaphysical
I stir in my skin for the taste of her mouth
Honeysuckle lips, too sweet for perceiving
Longing for candies, candles and crème
I indulge in love with passion wholehearted
Together everlasting as the works of a master
Never causing lament, my greatest performance

Wake to my Love

She left me overawed like the Baroque styles of Rome
Shall I applaud or be grateful when we are home
Tender skinned she lay in influence
How we sinned with much puissance
The small of her back, provocative dimples
I grow tall and cutback to curves, so simple
As the sun disappears only sleep will cumber
She's the one I will kiss as I wake from slumber

Cellular Love

As we speak to sunrises my ears never grow tired.
Enthralled in your explanations.
I hang on words as if your lips were cliffs.
To miss a sentence and fall to my death.
You charge through me.
Like currents of an electric eel.
Waves of voltage and circuit board dynamics.
Microphones and speakers broadcast my imagination.
If only our distance was relative.
We'll speak again tomorrow.

Unbounded Rapture

Theretofore my purged desire
Lips and butterflies overwhelm
Iniquity, lust and mania filled souls
Tender and truculent an absurd medley
Quenched pining, indignation evanesce
Delusion to substance, serenity anon

Hyperbolize

His demeanor over laden with tribulation
Fighting equilibrium as tensions mount
Forbearance nay chastity
Smoke rolls and struggles digress
Once cringing with bloodlust
He now sleeps like a babe

Haiku's

Absolute

She calms my being
Once unruly, rambunctious
Together we're one

12/21/12

It's the end of days
Utilize and takes a nap
I dream of nature

Lost Love

Kiss me softly love,
burning hearts course with feeling,
forgotten comfort.

Muse

O gentle wisdom
Creativity inspired
Tranquil devotion

While you Smile

Her kenpeckled lips
Loud with passionate shimmer
Calmed, I count my boon

Confusion to Clarity

(Double Haiku)

Disoriented
Stumbled thoughts mimic my steps
I will ascertain

O sweet clairvoyance
Lost enigma's unravel
The boggle of gods

Made in the USA
Coppell, TX
07 October 2021